Human Ignorance:
From A to Z

By Dustin Minor

Published by

4 Paws
Games and
Publishing

Bruno, Saskatchewan, Canada

www.4-Paws-Games-and-Publishing.ca

Human Ignorance: From A to Z

Written by Dustin Minor

Cover Art by Dave A.

Edited by Kourtnie Mckenzie & 4 Paws Games and Publishing

Formatted and Published by 4 Paws Games and Publishing

First publication

Published May 2019

ISBN-13: 978-1-988345-96-3

Published by 4 Paws Games and Publishing

P.O. Box 444

Humboldt, Saskatchewan, Canada S0K 2A0

http://www.4-Paws-Games-and-Publishing.ca

FBI ANTI-PIRACY WARNING

HUMAN IGNORANCE: FROM A TO Z

No society is perfect; utopia simply does not exist. But that doesn't mean people didn't try to figure out how to achieve it. Plato's Republic (370-360 B.C.), for example, is a series of books that detail one of the earliest conceptions of a utopian society, most likely written during the Peloponnesian War. Topics covered include the definition of "justice," different forms of government and so on. Texts and ideas that followed include Islands of the Sun by Iambulus (165-50 B.C.), The Peach Blossom Spring by Tao Yuanming (421 C.E.) and The Virtuous City by Al-Farabi (874-950). More texts appeared during the 16th and 17th centuries, continuing to appear until the present day, with one of the most recent examples being 2016's Ecotopia 2121: A Vision of Our Future Green Utopia by Alan Marshal, which documents the supposed improvements various cities could take on over the next century.

Within each society, we should not miss some faults. As you can imagine, everyone has a different idea for what works and what doesn't. We are not perfect. Not you, nor me, not as singular parts or a grouping that is unified. However, there are certain acts, crimes, and attitudes that pose glaring detriments to society, both to the largest masses and the smallest units. What you are about to read will list a few, from A to Z, and provide possible solutions for each issue. Sadly, there isn't one panacea for all woes. Not all of these might even be the objectively right choice. But it should generate thoughts and present viewpoints from which we can assess the issues. So, get comfortable, prepare yourself some tea or hot chocolate, clean those reading glasses and keep optimistic. We might be here for a while.

A is for ageism, which Webster dictionary defines as, "prejudice or discrimination against a particular age-group and especially the elderly." An example would be assuming that someone is incapable of something because they are "too old." Another subtler example is speaking up or raising your voice around an elderly person, whether you know of their hearing capabilities. Said person may be able to hear you at your normal register and volume, but some would increase it, based on their assumption of the elderly person in question. This can even be to the point that a person does not even need to be a part of the elderly, but simply look such. For example, young people who have white hair, perhaps just because of a birth defect, but not due to their age, may experience this because of an assumption of age and hearing capabilities.

Is this a bad thing? Potentially. While it is true that those of the elderly persuasion would prefer that you speak up and not to mention it (Aging Care, Life Hacker), the issue comes in when negative connotations are assigned to it. That is, the assumption that an individual more on in years is "less than" and to be only left at that. There are considerations to keep for sure. Whether they're hard of hearing or suffer from a physical or mental condition so characteristic of old age, it's more productive to work around these hindrances and try to meet the other halfway, so to speak. And even then, not every part of aging needs a stigma when it comes to "going gray."

But ageism is not exclusive to the elderly; young people experience it, too. For example, the right to vote is exclusive to members above the age of 18 in the United States of America. Now I'm not saying we should let small, not-potty-trained toddlers decide anything in the government.

But I am saying that there is no magic number that can decide when you are old enough to make important decisions. It just doesn't work that way. After all, in the age-old story, the first step to solving a problem is admitting that you've got one. But to those who find this example too extreme, here's another: children are the only population that can legally be hit in any developed first world country. There are still people advocating even more of an ability to harm minors as punishment, also known as corporal punishment. They swear by the method, even though there is a mountain of evidence against it.

A is also for Ableism, the discrimination in which the able-bodied are favored over disabled. This is a most important issue, because not everyone is capable of the same things. I am hard of hearing, Bipolar Type One, Schizoaffective Disorder, Clinically Depressed, am afflicted with an Anxiety Disorder and Hydrocephalus. It's near impossible to find someone willing to put up with all of that to hire me. I was born with all this. It's in my genes. Do I deserve to die alone under a bridge once I run out of people willing to help me because of things I cannot do? Ask yourself that.

B is for bigotry. There is no 100% correct way to run the world, or any country. We as unique humans possess unique opinions. Therefore, no one is always right or always wrong. The only way to truly live is with honest collaboration, and the enemy to that is bigotry. You are not the center of the universe, and you are not always right just because you want to be. You might not agree with the things that some people do, but so long but so long as they give you, as well as others, the space that human rights grant all of us, you have no reason to say they aren't allowed to do whatever it is they're doing. We're not defined as gay people, straight people, tall people, short people, black people, white people, Muslims, Mexicans, Chinese, Japanese, Middle Easterners, Somalis, Indians, and a multitude of other titles. We are all just people.

We are all human beings, Homo sapiens, humans. You know, sometimes I infer we take that last one — the human race — too seriously. Possibly it's because we all seem to have faith that life is a race to make the most money and seem the most impressive. But what I imagine it means is that life and human existence is a race against time, not other humans, to make the earth, and all it offers, the most wonderful thing in all of space before it is inevitably destroyed by something in the future. That goal only can and only will ever be achieved by full cooperation of all of us.

C is corruption. In Government, in private companies, in common people, in everyone. Now, let me be clear, there are many people who genuinely do things for good reasons. But it is all too common for people to only be looking out for themselves. Lying, cheating, foul play, it's all commonplace in our world now. It need not be, though. We all possess the option to promote honesty and transparency. Together we possess the ability to make the world a better place by making kinder people within ourselves. It may seem an impossible task, but when one counts to a million, the number you start with is one, is it not? You only need to be willing to be that one that starts the trend. We may never fully eliminate the evil, but we can rise to challenge it!

C is also for Conformity. "A nation of sheep shopping run by pigs" Said Edward R. Murrow. I find such things to be true, but not just in a political sense. We conform every day to Societal Norms we make up ourselves. Boys wear blue, girls wear pink. Men wear suits, women wear dresses. Caucasians own businesses, Latinos clean houses of Caucasians, and African as well as Native Americans do drugs while living in ghettos. All homeless people are homeless because they waste their money on drugs and alcohol, which is why we are not obligated to help them—they will throw that help away anyhow. There are many more ways to conform, and the vast majority do. It is sad because all these things listed above are not true; it is only a socially acceptable form of over-generalization.

A final C, very important to me, is this:

Contradiction. Meaning to say something, then say something that in any way goes against the previous statement.

I will admit my own guilt of contradictions may arise in this very book, but wherever you find it, it is the cause of learned culture and bias; and I do not want learned culture and bias to be the takeaway from this book. The takeaway from this book, should you read this far, is another C. A positive one.

Change. I hope the world changes for the better because of my writing this book. I realize it's a long shot, but I was taught to reach for the stars (despite being so short).

I only want to help.

Next is **D** for many things, but let's talk about a personal one to me. Discrimination. You can't tell a person who they are or what they'll be. It's not right and if it happened to you, you would see. Well, perhaps not because it undoubtedly has already. Don't believe me? I'll prove it. To all the guys, how many times were you told to stop crying?

Girls, how many times were you told to act like a lady? Non-binaries, how many times were you told you were a liar, or that your community doesn't really exist, and you're just attention seekers or something of that sort? Discrimination is not just about skin color, though that's still bad too, and common. It's supposed to be frowned upon, but it's just discrete. Sometimes not even that.

It is everywhere, yet it need not be.

We can choose to eliminate it with collaboration and kindness.

It would be hard, but possible. We can do it.

E is empathy or rather, the lack thereof. You see it is imperative to human society for all to possess the ability to get into someone else's shoes and feel what they feel. Humanity is often self-centered, speaking. Many suffer, few care, and even fewer step up to make things better.

How do I know?

Strength in numbers. If we had large numbers trying to solve a problem, they would solve it. Like with Polio. But sadly, there are people who oppose seeking solutions for various reasons. Most of these reasons are religious or personal, at least from my experience, but I do not judge, for a judge I am not.

But back to the point, nothing—or at most, very little—gets done to solve things like poverty and hunger, because the majority do not wish to spend the resources or the time to end it, because that means less resources and time for themselves, regardless of whether it is needed for their survival.

We need to learn that it is okay to feel, to share, to care, and to love. Something we will never achieve with the current societal mentality of kill or be killed, and anything different is bad. All things are basically condemned if it is outside of what is socially normal. The reality is that the only time "kill or be killed" applies (metaphorically speaking) is when you are even able to be killed in the first place.

For example, whoever is currently CEO of McDonald's® is set for life. Sure, he must work, but he will never need to worry about where his next meal comes from (probably not from McDonald's® because he can afford not to rely on fast food), nor will he worry where he will sleep that night. Retirement plans and college funds for any kids they might have are already set in place and will not change unless something drastic happens to the business, something so devastating, it wiped out McDonald's® across the globe for good.

But still in the US alone 25% of the country is chained in poverty, 22% of which have jobs and work like everyone else. This is not ethical; there is an imbalance of fairness.

Of course, I've heard all my life that "life isn't fair."

Well, maybe it ought to be.

It could be, if only we would all wisen up, put aside our differences, and collaborate. Empathy is so important, I'd almost dare say it's everything when it comes to running a country. It's why I'd never run for president. Why would I want a job where I'm scrutinized, where the fate of millions of lives, both in my country and out, can at least partially rest on my shoulders, and no matter what I do, a large group of people will hate me for doing what I believe is right, and some may even want me dead for it?

Aside from government matters, empathy is important in everyday lives. I can almost guarantee the suicide rate would go down if more people believed that someone cared for them, even just one other person, one human connection. That can make all the difference between a noose or a college degree to many people.

I understand that many who died of their own hand did have people that cared, and to those loved ones, I'm sorry for your loss—because, it is a loss. He or she was important to you, and to the world, they just didn't understand it, and it is not your fault that they could not see it, nor is it theirs. But if we, as a society, cared more for each other, I can almost guarantee it would happen less.

A chain reaction would occur, people who need help would get it, others would not be bullied into needing that help in the first place, less would be afraid of the mentally ill—because the mentally ill would not be afraid of the stigma that wouldn't be as existent to seek help—and crime would go down, sincere there would be little to no desperation for anything. We would all have a baseline, like a trampoline, and on such, we could all rise with a mighty leap.

Well, not all of us; it is insane to insist we can save everyone. We can't save everyone, but we can save more than we do now. If we are not doing all we can, then we are only tragically wasting lives. Lives that are valuable; not to be wasted. Lives that complete our puzzle called life and humanity. We are losing important people every day. Ones we would not lose if we were to look inside of ourselves for the answers, because the only answer to pain is love, and the only way to die is pain. You will not be granted eternal life, but you will be granted a fuller one. We need to say, "You are allowed to love the world, and the world will love you if you let it."

But I digress.

On to the letter **F**, and it's a good one: F is for facts.

We must all state facts instead of saying just what would rile up the consumer the most. We need rules, not ratings. Hardcore facts. I am not Donald Trump; I do not accept that all news is made up, or at least the ones that talk bad about me, but I understand that facts are twisted sometimes, and that needs to stop. It would only benefit people to realize the truth and not just what scares them into reading more. I advocated for the benefit of everyone. I personally would go to the news story that is the truest, and not just the most shocking. So, I encourage an honesty only policy in everything and everyone in every place at every time. Because the truth is powerful, it can, it should, and it will prevail through all.

We cannot be a functioning society with trickery and misdirection, only with trust and honesty. Factual information can only achieve this, it's swift distribution, and unlimited access to that information. No government interference, and not making things up to make it more interesting. No trying to lie to readers, instead of telling them the truth, so they will read your story instead of some other source's story. My suggestion to achieve such a thing is to make the most quality in your work, making it easy to read or watch. You need not fabricate things to make them interesting, but you can entice people with the quality of what you do, rather than making all of it, or even some of it, up. The only interpretation should be the true interpretation, but you can tell the truth in many ways with many words. But what matters is that you tell the truth.

F is also for forgiveness, which we as a human race need to learn to show more. Everybody makes mistakes. This could be saying the wrong thing accidentally or bullying on purpose. Either way, people may end up sorry for what they did, and that remorse needs to be accepted and respected, even if their mistake, whether purposeful, is not forgotten. Because if no one forgives, and everybody just stay labeled as what they previously did in the past, then they will never be able to move on to a better future. And by relation, neither will you. You will always be filled with the hate of past transgressions, and carry it around with you, wherever you go. Too often, you may use that to prejudge people of similar qualities, who may, to your surprise, be decent people. Therefore, you would have none of the positive experiences you may have had with them. You could also have an infinite number of possibilities to grow in almost every way.

To appeal to the more possibly conservative audience, imagine making a business partner of your old high school bully and you both make millions, or even possibly becoming the most financially successful partnership. That would never happen if you were to never forgive them enough to work with them. I, at least, don't see how you could.

G is for global warming, and like it or not, we are a major contributor to it. We are the cause, the solution, and the only prevention. But first we must all admit to our crimes and believe it exists, for we cannot fight a foe until we fully acknowledge it's there. We must all see it and we must all fight. This is the one and only planet we've got, and we may not get another, or at the least we should not. Because if we do not take care of this one, then what does that speak of the next? If we do not learn our lesson now, the next planet would share the same fate and we would have nowhere to go.

Unless there's another planet which we will also trash, but what is the point of going through all the trouble to get to another, if we can learn here and now? —instead we could keep this planet for generations, if we only take care of it, as it takes care of us.

Our planet provides us with our home, we provide it with trash. We kill the thing that provides us life, and is necessary, because we are too selfish to realize that we could be doing anything wrong. We all want to believe that we are absolute good, but that is not the truth. Most of us do not mean harm but we know not what we do. We only see what they tell us, and right now we are told that global warming is a hoax invented by the Chinese. By our very own current president, as I write this in 2017. President Donald J. Trump fully believes that global warming only exists to affect his golf course, but when it comes to everything else, he believes — and has some nation convinced — that global warming is a fraud. With that kind of mindset, we will never save ourselves. We are doomed.

However, this need not be the case; we can change ourselves and the world. But first we need to realize that it is necessary

H is for hierarchy. I do not speak to governments with this system, but to modern society who, for some reason, still believes in this. By that I mean there's always someone that maintains that they're better than everyone else, and there are always people who are made to believe that they are worse than everyone else, whether it's true. This is the way my country and, as far as I know, the world works. It is believed for there to be someone on the top, there need to be people below them. And for there to even be a top, there must be a bottom.

We treat our own kind this way, as if we never evolved beyond slavery.

No one is better than anyone else; everyone just has different skills. These skills may help you improve your life but makes no one better or worse than you. You only have yourself to work with, and so does everyone else. You cannot physically be any different from who you are, so there's no point in making others conclude they must be. Once you get to the top of the pyramid, you'll be there alone. To be the best is to only use the people under you as a way to get there. I speak not to people who worked their way to the top, but at the same time, I do. Because I know you most likely didn't do it without help.

H also stands for hate. Hate is everywhere and is a natural enemy of love. But hate need not win the war. It can't. Because, while these ideals may only seem tangible in fictional stories, I truly am faithful that love conquers all or— at the very least—has the potential to prevail, if you let it. There is no reason that hate conquer loves, other than our willingness to let it do so. But we need not go this way; we can love. There is another way. A better way.

We can all come together in love and rise against the hate.

We can choose. You can choose.

No one has to be a target. Hate can end.

We can all hold each other as a family and make sure no one is ever left out again.

I is for inequality. There is no good reason that any person should be treated any differently from any other person. Yet to this day it still happens, everywhere, every day, all the time. It need not be this way; inequality only exists because we let it exist. We choose to treat others differently based on the stereotypes we learned from others. But we don't have to continue this behavior. We can change the world for the better to make sure that inequality can never happen again. No one should be barred from having something that someone else has, or from doing what someone else can do. This includes, but is not limited to: marriage; owning a home; renting a home; having a job; being able to be served as a paying customer in any public place; being able to buy a product as a paying customer in any public store; being able to have health insurance; being able to have or adopt children; only being arrested for a crime you actually committed, and then getting a fair, speedy trial after; using a restroom; taking care of the children by staying home, and/or working; and so on. Many things that are unfair in this world need not be, yet we choose to let them be unfair. The world can be fair, if we let it, if we make it. We made the world unfair, and we can make it fair again.

J is for Justice, or at least the twisted idea we possess on its name. Just because the conclusion is reached does not mean it is the correct one. The innocent have been punished and the guilty have gotten away with their crimes. Tampered, damaged, or even hidden evidence, false testimonies, corrupt judges, attorneys, prosecutors, and jury members, inaccurate methods of obtaining evidence, racial profiling, etcetera, are all ways someone innocent can be punished, while someone guilty gets away. May I say that it is very unbecoming of a nation, that a factor of whether you fear the police or feel protected around them is the color of your skin. I know this is an example that many do not believe in, and that see this as a tired tale, but it is very real. And true justice can only come from cooperation, open-mindedness, and love and respect for each other as fellow human beings. It will be a hard-won battle, but it can be won.

I understand many would be concerned about the possibility of the guilty going free. But they already are. They need rehabilitation, not eternal incarceration. And no matter the sentence, it is essentially eternal, as most prisoners do eventually return to jail a multiple times throughout their lives. Ex-convicts are discriminated against and treated as lesser. It's like a punishment that never ends. It's hard to get a job regularly, from first-hand experience. I have never been arrested, but if I had a record, I could kiss my chances goodbye depending on the offense. It needs to be taught that what they are doing is morally wrong—at least, if it is wrong; some laws are ridiculous. — Once the lesson is over, it should not have any further effect on their life. Some may want revenge, but a wise man once said: "An eye for an eye, and the whole world goes blind." Vengeance solves nothing, as we'll explore more later. Holding over punishments for bad behavior makes more bad behavior in rebellion.

K is for killers. Killing is bad, but it does not stem from bad people, simply good people who make bad decisions or are forced to make those bad decisions. For example, if you needed to choose between the life of yourself and someone else — either by them directly attacking you, so that you must defend yourself, or by someone forcing you to kill for them, or else they get you— you're confronted with a bad decision. I have heard of both scenarios. Killing or committing any crime that involves only the mentally sound happens only in those forced to do it, either by their current circumstances, or in what they conclude is a situation of fight or flight. They would never commit a crime without some outer influence.

Say a wife kills a cheating husband who she catches in bed with another woman, whom she also murders. If the husband did not cheat, he and the other woman would be alive. Now I do not justify the murder in that scenario—that man did not deserve to die simply for being unhappy in a marriage—but we must admit cause-and-effect, not label her a bad woman. That accomplishes nothing. What we want is to get her to a healthy place in society, so that this does not happen again, and so she can continue to contribute the growth of the society in which she lives.

L is for labels, and labels are for objects, not humans. While they have their uses, and should by no means be eradicated from language — unlike a lot of other things I have and will talk about in this book — we should not use them so religiously to define people; and on the other side of the discussion, we should respect when they do, or don't, want certain labels to be used.

Labels exist because somebody thousands of years ago, and continuing to present day, made up that defining word.

The catch is, you don't need to use them. I recall a book from my childhood, "Frindle" by Andrew Clements. The reason I bring this up is the plot of it. A boy and his friends try to popularize a new word for a pen, a frindle. I remember vaguely that others fought against their efforts, being corrected by teachers and whatnot, to use the socially acceptable word, "pen." Yet the part that I am referencing is the fact that, nowhere along the way — even after the new word is acknowledged and accepted—do they force anyone to use it, nor do they ridicule anyone who doesn't use it. It is simply treated as a fun new word to add spice to the language, nothing more, nothing less, and that is just fine.

So why do we, as a society, force people to conform to what we think, when they are them, and we are us? It is not us versus them, it is humanity. That's all. Beyond that, every label is entirely made up to fit the culture of its location, and where you are should not define who you are or how you're seen, only you should determine that. Because only you truly can.

M is for money, and that includes all currencies, throughout history, as well as across the world. The obsession people have with it, the amount of people who can't make enough of it, and the amount of people who inherit all they need to survive, then abuse those who need to work beyond healthy means: this is an imbalance of power in an unprecedented form. People die because of this imbalance, alone, and with no hope to ever have a better life. People are starving around the world not for lack of resources, but for lack of access to those resources, because of the greed of others who don't necessarily need them. The system we use is broken, and it leaves many people without reliable access to shelter, food, and water, while with others it leaves a large excess with extravagant non-essentials. It's not proportional, and it needs to be stopped. No one should starve so someone else can be rich. But everyone should be able to make their livelihood as well; we should be able to work, and seek fulfillment, without it costing others.

M is also for media. In books, movies, websites, video games, TV, magazines, news reports—media can be corrupt, no matter the source. It's a game of money and keeping attention and numbers. How many sold? How long did they watch? What is the rating on [insert website here]? The fact that media can influence other media so drastically, in any way fathomable, is what makes it dangerous. The world becomes a giant game of telephone, and it's difficult to discover truth from fact; which means misinformation is pervasive.

In my schooling, teachers and books reiterated many times: we need to look at multiple sources to find the information we need; cross-reference it with other sources to make sure it all matches; and consider the logical fallacies in that media. But everyone should be—if they are not already—asking, why is the information allowed to be different depending on what article you pick? That answer is beyond me.

N is for narcissist. I realize that this is a recognized mental disorder, and I encourage all who possess the affliction to seek professional help. But there are those who just illusion themselves that they are above others for illegitimate reasons. For those people, this is a message for you.

There is no single person on earth whose importance outweighs everyone, or even anyone else but themselves. We are all human biologically, and though we have independent strengths and weakness, each of us is fundamentally human. We should treat each other as such. It is our right and duty to make sure that everyone, regardless of any circumstance, reaches their full potential in their time on this planet. To do anything less is to waste your own time on the planet. The only true hindrance of growth is personal. You cannot and will not stop a determined heart from rising if it truly wants to.

O is for over-generalization, the assumption that because one person contains similarities to other people, that they can be grouped together. Grouping can happen based on single-minded, single cause-and-effect fallacious reasoning, rather than considering the well-rounded person, or the variables leading to an event. For example, the stereotype that persons of color all like chicken—I have no idea who started that, but it is not true. — On the other end of the spectrum, not all Caucasians like country music. I personally know a fair number of the fair-skinned who hate that genre. Race, age, intelligence, physical ability, appearance, and many other assumptions, often cultivate themselves into overgeneralized stereotypes that divide us. In reality though, we are each unique. Conversely, we are also similar in ways many overlook. We are all human, regardless if from the United States of America, the United Kingdom, Syria, Israel, or elsewhere. We are also individualistic, regardless of where we grew up. This needs to be recognized in order for us to grow as not just separate countries, but as a world as a whole. We need to come together as individuals making a whole.

P stands for pedophilia. It should never be allowed, not in any country, city, or place. It is immoral at a fundamental level, one of the baselines of an ethical society. But it is also not black and white, at least in my eyes.

Pedophilia is defined as sexual urges toward prepubescent children. With this I have two qualms. The first being, how do you define a child? In the USA it is any person or persons under the magical age of 18. Age of consent laws vary from state to state within, but the age of 18 is generally what is accepted. Yet in other cultures around the world, you are an adult sometimes as young as 15, sometimes even younger. That makes the line a bit blurred to me. It makes the definition of pedophilia change based on your location and the culture within that place.

I maintain that the ability to give or deny consent has no magical age. Even some older than 18 are honestly not prepared to consent to sex, and are also, in some cases, unable to deny consent for various reasons. But I have also seen younger teenagers able to make informed decisions and have healthy sexual relations with their chosen partners.

Some cultures contain relations between much older adults and very young children. This I will not comment on, as each culture is different, and I do not wish to slander any. But I only want to put out there, that the ability to consent is not so black and white as one might hold true, like it or not. At one point it was acceptable and even encouraged for girls as young as 12, or just after the start of maturity, to settle, marry, and have children, never mind just be sexually intimate.

Remember how I said I had two qualms? Here's my second one: I don't know how all the world has their justice system regarding punishing pedophiles. I come from a US standard. But I have a problem with it. If the offenders are shunned from the community, what incentive do they have to change and become better people? Or incentive to, at the very least, not repeat or do an even worse offense? Society hates them already upon the first offense, making their lives infinitely harder to live. That only drives to even more crimes like theft, as no one will hire them. They will be unable to make a living—and be forced into a life of crime—all because of one bad choice to act on an urge. It is an illness which many are afflicted with and do not want, yet seeking treatment is met with backlash. Some may argue they do not want to change, so treatment has no value; but no human inherently wants to hurt another. Some pedophiles are predators because, as children, they were also sexually assaulted, and they may respond to therapy; while others were born with deficiencies that would require more long-term care — but even then, rehabilitation offers hope, whereas incarceration is a dead-end with no answers. This is a problem that can be dealt with by therapy instead of jail, and I maintain it ought to be. I personally conclude a change needs to happen, because if just throwing criminals in jail was ever going to solve a crime, it would have long ago, but crime keeps happening.

Q is a quandary, a dilemma, a problem, or general state of uncertainty. What does this have to do with humanity? The fact that there are so many quandaries, but so few solutions or people working together to find them. Some things are rumored to not be attempted at being solved are already completed but hidden by the government for monetary reasons. I hear it all the time, that no one is researching cancer or diabetes and other things, or that the answer is found, but too much money is made off the current treatment to these diseases to justify releasing a cure. I don't know if it's true, but if it is, shame on the ones doing this. Until we're able to build a bridge between everyday people, the latest research, and Big Pharma, we'll continue to worry about what's going on behind medical doors.

Every four years, during the presidential election, neighbors become enemies, friends become foes. For several months we watch ads in swing states and learn misinformation. We act like the President is the end-all be-all, when the Senate, House, and Supreme Court are just as powerful. The other branches can remove the President from power if necessary, or at least stop his actions if they are deemed to be unconstitutional. Knowing who you are putting in office is important but knowing who you put in all the offices of government is imperative. Maybe if the other branches were taken more seriously, there would be fewer quandaries around the world.

R is for rape culture, a touchy subject for many reasons.

First and foremost, I want to give a personal apology to all the victims, including those who have been previously falsely accused and all who ever will, the victims of the actual violence, and the families of both the previously mentioned parties. If you are a victim of any type of assault, and your assailant was not convicted, our system has failed you. If you are a victim of being falsely accused of any type of assault, our system has also failed you. I am deeply sorry, and I regret that the current system could not help you.

To the offenders, you did wrong, but I'm sure you know that and do not need me to tell you. You may or may not be punished. Either way, you need to change. That's all that really matters in the end. You need to make the choice and the effort to change, but just know that there is someone who knows you can. Me. You might not be able to make it up to the person you hurt, but you can make yourself a better person and never hurt anyone again. These are the ideas we need to instill into today's people. When you make someone a criminal in the United States of America, you make them scum, incapable of change and unhireable in many cases. No way to get a job means needing to resort to theft and robbery, leading to more crime and victims and violence and vengeance. This cycle of abuse does no good for the victims or the offenders. Many conclude justice is punishing and forgetting, but you cannot truly forget until you forgive; in forgiving, you can move on.

Another R is for religion. Religion is a positive, healthy thing for many people, and we should be allowed to practice beliefs with freedom—without persecution. But that does not mean that anyone should be allowed to impose their beliefs on society at large. Just because you are Catholic does not mean you can tell me not to be gay; it only means that you maintain you are not supposed to be gay. You can believe it is wrong of me to be gay, but your right to swing your arms ends where my nose begins. You cannot make me convert, just like I cannot make you an atheist. Not only because it is wrong, but because it is impossible. Conversion therapy only changes the conduct of a person, not their actual stance—that stays with them. A converted gay man may not lay with another man ever again, or want to, but fundamentally, he will still be gay. He can't change that and should not be punished for it. Religious beliefs should not cost someone the way they were meant to authentically live their life.

S is for sickness. We usually, but not always, acknowledge physical sickness. Now, still a substantial amount of the time, people will be fired for long-term physical illnesses as well, which is a problem. But at the moment, mental illness has a long way to reaching the level that physical illness is acknowledged.

For example, if you contracted pneumonia, you are usually safe to call off work, but if you are depressed, you are usually stuck going or are punished for skipping, unless you have disability benefits of some sort, or a doctor's note. Sometimes, that doesn't even help. This is never okay, under any circumstance. Mental illness is real, and it's on the rise throughout many societies. It plagues those old and young, and there is little protection for those afflicted in my country. Most of the homeless are made up of people with some type of mental illness or other disability, and they go untreated without health insurance. It is not right, and something must change. We need to accept and acknowledge mental illness and physical disability as serious situations, and that is the first step to change.

S is also for sexism, for everyone. Men are not monsters looking to assault every girl they see. And a lot of men who don't have the rights to see their kids should be able to see them. Men also shouldn't automatically be the ones to pay child support. If the world were fair, no one would need to pay child support or alimony, because everyone would make enough money, anyway. I aspire for that. But on to women. Wearing shorts or a skirt is okay, yet it doesn't make touching okay. Women can do work just as well as men, so they should not be shorted on jobs or pay because of their born sex. Furthermore, no sex should feel pressured to alter any part of themselves because of the culture of where they are or anyone else. Everyone should be themselves. Men and women should be able to alter their bodies as they please, without causing permanent harm to themselves or others. If it hurts no one, go ahead. Get circumcised or pierced, or not if you want, or whatever other unconventional form of art you want on your body. But only if you want it in your heart, for yourself. Outside pressure must cease in the form of many things, sexism only one of them. It must stop for the betterment of all.

T is for Transphobia. No, that woman in the women's room is not going to harm your child because she was previously a he. Though in my eyes she was never a he. All trans women are real women to me, and as far as I should care, have been all their lives. If there's a person desperate enough to dress as a woman to go in the women's room to harm someone, would they not be desperate enough to just go in as themselves without it? Why would they need to? It's the same risk if they get caught, anyway. As a man or woman, they would be persecuted for their crime. No one would believe that they were just a transitioning person in the bathroom while they were in the act, would they? I hope not. Though it might not be as obvious to see as I conclude. Nevertheless, the sign on the door, and level of security around it, does not make a force field impenetrable by predators. The only way to protect the men, women, and children of our country—if that is the true reason for the issue with the restroom—is to teach the children that it is wrong to hurt others in any sense for any reason, including gender.

Another issue is that there are less or differing services and jobs available to trans* persons. Why is this even an issue? Whatever gender, or lack thereof, a person identifies as, does not make you a better employee or customer. Saying that it is an insult to God is just ludicrous. Once again, you lose the right to swing your arms where my nose begins. Either way, I'm sure even God had this in his plans, (if there is a God to have a plan, I don't personally know,) but perhaps there is a reason the trans* persons are the way they are. Perhaps they're here to change the world, to evolve us as a species. Has no one considered that? Few I've met even thought about it.

U is for the underprivileged. The homeless man on the street begging for food is spat on and told to get a job, but here's what those people saying those hurtful words don't realize. If you can't shower, change clothes, travel, prove a home address and ID, or don't possess work experience, it can be impossible to get a job, let alone one that will allow them to get themselves off their feet. Such an expectation is ridiculous. People aren't just handing out jobs in the United States of America, and if they were, who's to say they wouldn't have your job? You might owe having a job to someone else being poor. So, you should take care of the homeless who can't care for themselves, because they just might be taking care of you.

V is two things, vengeance, and violence. Violence is never necessary; it usually stems from anger and in retaliation or defense from other violence. No one should get angry enough to hurt another. That shows a lack of control and dignity. That lack of control, or even dignity, can stem from a mental problem, but it's not always that way. You allowed this person so much power in your head by getting angry, if you think about it. In fact, that's how you're forfeiting power to them—by thinking. If you are angry at someone, you are thinking about them, most likely a lot. They are in your thoughts. Why would you allow them to place themselves there if you don't like them? As for retaliation or defense: if the first person were never violent, the cycle of violence would not have occurred; so, it's that deeper root that needs to be addressed.

Vengeance usually stems from violence; but what good does revenge do? Does it make you feel better? perhaps for a short while. But it won't make you happy forever. Short-term gains will destroy long-term growth. You only hurt a person, and in the long run, yourself. By burning a bridge, instead of trying to reconnect and forgive, you make it harder on yourself. A lot of things are done accidentally. You could lose a potential or past friend if you let pain consume you with anger. Stop, think, and breathe. Not everything requires an immediate reaction. You can take your time when making decisions. Do you really want to burn this bridge? If not, the answer to the two V's is the most powerful positive L in the world: love.

W is for welfare. I speak from a US-of-A perspective, I state once again. We are not doing enough for those on welfare; there are too many homeless persons here. Too many people are in a situation they can't escape, because of everyone telling them to just get out of it, while no one is willing to help. Everyone needs food, water, and shelter; wouldn't it be better to make sure everyone had those? I'm not suggesting a communism — not that any form of government is bad; any government can be good or bad, depending on how it's run — but if everyone had what they needed, then everyone would possess what they need and work for what they want; just as I am working to write this book, because that is what I want to work towards. I don't need to struggle working a dead-end job I don't want because I need to eat or hide from rain. And if you're worried about what would happen to people who work those unfavorable jobs, make them favorable. Fair pay, benefits, time off, the works. But most importantly, be good to the employees; make the stigma of being rude to an employee as societal a scandal as not tipping your pizza guy. Shift the perspective from "the customer is always right" to "customers and employees are human beings sharing a planet together." And stop making the bulk of server wages their tips. The less people feel desperate, the more we thrive.

X is for xenophobia or "an irrational intense dislike, hatred, or fear of people from other countries." I speak to the world this time when I say this. I find it highly improbable, probably impossible, that you have no one in your family line from another country. What's the point of being afraid of people from other countries? They were born in the same fashion you were and the same basic needs to water, food, and shelter. What's to be afraid of inherently that you can say of the whole country of people without overgeneralizing a stereotype? Probably not much. There is no reason. They are human just like you, and I'm sure if you are friendly to all, you will receive the same from the vast majority. A few bad apples do not spoil the whole tree.

Y is for youth. Today our young get up bright and early in the morning—actually, I take that back, it's not always bright; but it is almost always early— typically go to school, do after-school activities they may or may not want to do, come home, do homework, do chores, and do their own thing, if they have time. A lot of people don't for several reasons. Too much homework and school work, too many after-school activities, too many chores. Let me ask you, where is the part where they are a kid?

Even if they are not a kid anymore at first glance—like let's say, someone 17—so they cannot vote; they are not recognized by the state as an adult yet; yet parents take every opportunity to remind them that they will be adults soon, when Timmy hasn't picked up his socks. Parents will pressure their children — "why does he live like this," "he wasn't raised this way," "he will never get anywhere in life"— because he just won't learn to pick up his darned socks! This is a real thing lots of teens endure, and the age it starts gets younger all the time. I speak from experience. It's worse when you have older and younger siblings who parents use as measuring sticks.

"Jade doesn't do this."

"Do you see what Greg did? Why can't you be more like him?"

It's this kind of pressure that is poisonous to development. I didn't do it like him because I am not him. I am not perfect, nobody is. But we act like such a thing exists, and it's hurting our future generation, some even to the point of suicide. We as a society need to work together to protect the youth and make sure no one feels they need to go to that extreme. We need to teach people are beautiful, and the world is beautiful, even if it has faults.

Everyone has faults. No one is alone.

Z is for zealotry. Zealotry, according to Merriam-Webster, is defined as an excess of zeal or fanatical devotion. Zealotry is commonly associated with religious or political extremists. Perhaps you already have thoughts of terrorism in your head, suicide bombers, innocent victims beheaded on live television. Or possibly you see of some mangy man standing atop a soap box, proclaiming that the end is near, and it's time to repent. Sources on why zealots are the way they are were not easy to come by, but an article from Psychology Today might have the answer. In "Fanaticism is a Disease like Alcoholism," Jeremy E. Sherman likens the religious and political fanatics to drunk drivers. He says that there's a know-it-all attitude and having the pride and final word is addictive, but there are a great many deal of people that can get hurt when they act like this even if the fanatic concludes they're perfectly fine. The writer even drafted a 12-step program named "Fanatics' Anonymous" and centered the steps around letting go of the fanatic ideologies and embracing reason. For example, raping and murdering a trans person is not reasonable. But debating with your friend on a political and religious issue will most likely be a lot more reasonable because it's a more mindful and benevolent interaction.

Perhaps this raises the question: If we are treating zealotry like alcoholism, is it then a mental illness? Well, I'll tell you this: Treating the zealot like a criminal isn't going to be effective, just as you would a mental illness patient. And to be honest, if you were already wondering about that parallel, you aren't the only one. The Scientific American released a piece in 2016 about being able to distinguish the two, "How Do You Distinguish between Religious Fervor and Mental Illness?" by Nathaniel P. Morris. He also agrees that fanaticism hampers one's ability to make rational decisions. Not only that, he and many of his colleagues had come across patients who hallucinate and claim to speak with God, which already makes the distinction difficult to make. In the end, he doesn't put himself in a place to judge the beliefs of others but focuses on getting treatment to who needs it. He does cite tests that can objectively tell if someone is at risk for a mental illness, such as B12 deficiency and brain chemistry, but maintains that there needs to be some more help. He is hopeful that help will come.

To add one final note, not all zealots are concerned with pleasing God. We have political zealots too, people who push propaganda; people who would murder another person who disagrees with them. You cannot burn gays on a stake. You cannot rape and murder trans* persons. You cannot kill for political gain. You cannot commit a crime of any sort. But most of all, you cannot justify doing any of this with any religious or political stance. It is ludicrous and wrong to mess with the lives of others for your own agenda, no matter the reason.

You should not just do whatever you want, no matter what, in the name of politics—or anything else. No matter what you stand for, no one should have to get hurt to make it happen. Terrorism is unnecessary. Extremism is unnecessary. I assure that if you spoke nicely and calmly, at least some would be willing to hear you out. I would.

Well, now you know your ABC's—won't you change the world with me?

AUTHOR'S NOTE

Thank you for reading this far and for reading my note. I would also like to thank Naomi Dennis and Cayden Kopp for helping me in the editing process. I would also like to thank one of the teachers in my early childhood who inspired me to become an author, Mrs. Cathy Hall. I love you to bits. Finally, I would like to thank my family for believing in me. My baby sister Mackenzie Michelle Minor, my baby brother Brian Scott Minor Junior, my father Brian Scott Minor Senior, my great aunt Bernadette Mclaughlin, my older sister Jada Riviera Ramsey, and my mother Michelle Dawn Scott for all their own personal contributions to help see this through. We did these together guys.

Now onto a more serious note. I wrote this book to challenge the norm and force people to think about something bigger than themselves, if only for a moment. This book is not meant to offend any persons or cultures in any way. You guys do you; just don't judge others for being them. And let's all do that together.

Let's love the world we live in and everyone in it.

-Dustin Minor

www.ingramcontent.com/pod-product-compliance
Lightning Source LLC
Chambersburg PA
CBHW060706280326
41933CB00012B/2323